NEW & SELECTE
1965 – 2005

Other books by David Sutton

Out on a Limb (Rapp & Whiting, 1969)
Absences and Celebrations (Chatto & Windus,1982)
Flints (Peterloo, 1986)
Settlements (Peterloo, 1991)
The Planet Happiness (Gruffyground Press, 1997)
A Holding Action (Peterloo, 2000)

NEW & SELECTED POEMS
1965 – 2005
DAVID SUTTON

First published in 2005
by Peterloo Poets
The Old Chapel, Sand Lane, Calstock,
Cornwall PL18 9QX, U.K.

A catalogue record for this book is available
from the British Library

ISBN   1-904324-17-7

Printed in Great Britain by
Antony Rowe Ltd, Chippenham, Wilts.

ACKNOWLEDGEMENTS (New Poems)

'Embassy', 'Heroic Ideal', 'Journal', 'Beyond', The Immigrants', 'The House' and 'The Craftsmen' have all appeared in *Acumen*.

'Cosmologies', 'Sixty', 'A Candle for Mr Sokolowski' and 'The Programmer's Tale' were entered in Peterloo poetry competitions and have appeared in the subsequent anthologies of prize-winning poems for the years 2000, 2002, 2003 and 2004.

'At Steep' was written for the occasion of Myfanwy Thomas's ninetieth birthday under the auspices of the Edward Thomas Fellowship.

For Anne and Anthony, who encouraged

CONTENTS

Out on a Limb (1969)

Absences and Celebrations (1982)

Flints (1986)

Settlements (1991)

A Holding Action (2000)

New Poems

OUT ON A LIMB
1969

The Tree of Frost

Frost was on our world when we awoke,
Had furred the fences, floured coke,
And hung above the meadows like white smoke,
    But cold, but cold.

Its bite when we went from the house was in the air,
A brittle silk cocooned dead leaf, and where
The world was winter-naked, frost had there
    Clothed it with cold.

For as we went across the silver park
A chestnut-tree was there, leafless and stark,
But like a candelabra in the dark
    Because the cold

Had turned it all to candles, made a wick
Out of each twig and stick
Coating it with this thick
    White wax of cold.

And delicately now,
Vestal in the darkness, every bough
Was burning silently, as if some vow
    Kept it from cold.

Almost I did not want to see the sun,
Knowing that by it this must be undone,
This crystal beauty turn to weeping, run
    Relieved from cold.

But you, my winter-candled chestnut-tree,
Frozen so clear into my memory,
May you be ever such a light to me
    In time of cold,

Teaching me that for all its winter days
The earth has not forgotten how to praise –
Teach me like you to stand so, so to blaze
    Against the cold.

Seaside Honeymoon

Walking today round the headland
We heard the hollow turbulence of the waves
Roaring under the rocks, and hand in hand
Descending egg-smooth boulders, found the caves.
When we came out the sunlight hurt my eyes
And now in the dark I see that dazzle still.
Bright shapes of a perpetual surprise
Meet and fulfil.

In the afternoon we watched the tide
Mount slowly to the rock-pools, saw the weed
Stir at the water's touch, while sea-birds cried
Flaking around us, coming in to feed.
Squadrons of light were moving out at sea,
Moving on the waves, intensely bright.
Night shall outride their silver cavalry,
But not this night.

Then in the evening we watched the island gig-race:
The sweat on the rowers' faces in the sun,
Puffs of air, patching the rippled surface
To smoothness, and the gigs gliding on.
They moved within a black and golden shadow,
In a timeless rhythm, thrust and follow through.
In the twilight the boats came home to harbour
And I to you.

Now in your body the tide is going out.
Over the shining flats the rivers run,
Leaving the golden thongweed to await,
Never denied, the sea's rejuvenation.
Now in the night my mind unfocussing
From brightness drifts to a great dark of sleep.
Still above the sea the white gulls wheeling
Cry to the deep.

Division

It is strange to think that to you I shall always be
Someone else, that however much we agree
In mind and body and however true
Our love may be, to you I am always you.

All men are islands, so it has been said.
But islands spring from the one ocean bed.
If the seas of our division rolled away,
What joined us might lie open to the day.

But then, what seamed and blasted wilderness
Might be uncovered, what contrariness,
What strange and stranded monsters. Better so
To keep the seas between us, not to know

What lies beneath what seems serenity,
Accepting that to you I am not me,
Content with what is visible above,
The green and fertile islands of our love.

The Flowers

Where others saw none, she would notice these,
The lost flowers of the speedwell in the grass,
White and blue, more delicate than porcelain,
The clear gay red of poor man's weather glass,
And on waste places mayweed after rain
Spreading its florets to the drying breeze.

Did they grow as things for her to notice,
Or was she there that she might notice them?
What did they mean, all those since childhood moments
When she stood gazing, as if root and stem
Had brought the flower to its shy existence
For her alone, as she was brought to this?

Too doubtful of the question for an answer
She was contented in her ignorance,
And afterwards, in her remembering,
The plants even attained a ghostly fragrance
Which was not theirs in any real spring.
And so in her they came at last to flower.

Two Trees

I saw where a crab-apple tree grew through a willow,
That was old and rotten, hanging above the river.
Its small lithe trunk matched perfectly a hollow
In the other's side; it clung there like a lover,
And all its branches were so twined around
And through the other's branches, one could say
Only by tracing both trunks to the ground
Which was the loveliness, which the decay.
And yet if the decay should die at last,
So should the loveliness be sure to follow
From having clung to it so long, so fast.
It was the crab that chose this way to grow,
It was the crab gave sweetness to the air.
The willow played its part, by standing there.

No Other Elegy

All his village went to the funeral.
I never knew him well enough, it was
    No grief of mine.
But there was something in his way of death,
His being engaged, his lying in the road
    With a broken spine,
That I could not get out of my mind. At least,
It stayed there for an evening, while I pondered
    Vaguely on Fate,
Remembering how once at school, when I'd won a race,
He came in as I was showering, saying 'God,
    You went up that straight
Like a bloody bomb.' Now he'd gone like a bomb,
And bloodily enough, his life exploding,
    That motor-bike
Smashing him back against a telegraph pole
(No one quite knew how) in the night. But no,
    Old women may like
To draw a premonition out of innocence,
But I would just record his words as a kindness
    Spoken to one he hardly knew
Who was beneath him. And I'm afraid it's not much
Of an elegy for his broken life, but still
    What there is, is true.

The Ripples

You troubled the still pool of my mind
Like a pebble dropped into it. And I was so
Intent on wondering whose was the hand
And what it was that made these ripples flow,
Outwards, questingly, as if to find
Something beyond themselves – how could I know

That into your mind too a stone had dropped?
It was the laws of motion in the end
That brought us into love. For as they touched
Our ripples hesitated, spread and widened,
Shivered to a singleness, then stopped.
Where now did the waters meet and blend?

In The Staff-Room

'...and Gillian Smith came in late. I was marking the register.
So I said to her, 'Where've you been?' And she said, 'It's my
                                                          Mum.
She's bad again.' I could see she was nearly crying,
So I said, 'Would it help to tell me?' She just shook her head,
Biting her lip, you know, in that way children have,
And suddenly there she was against my shoulder,
Sobbing her heart out. I can tell you, it nearly broke mine.
I've never felt a child cry like it, and all the while
She wouldn't say a word, or couldn't. In the end
I did just manage to get her to give one smile,
And Janey West, who'd been hopping about all the time
Saying, 'Please, Miss, shall I find her hymn number for her?'
Took her away. Tell me, what's wrong with her mother?'

'Multiple sclerosis,' said Rosemary.
'She's one of a family of five. The father looks after them.
The mother can't lift a finger. Literally.
She's in and out of hospital all the time.
We had a report on Gill. It said she was showing
'Separation symptoms,' wetting the bed,
Doing this mirror writing – you know, backwards –
And wandering round at playtimes on her own.'

'Oh. I see.' She knew she didn't see.
After a while she broke out fiercely though.
'It's awful. But what is there you can do?'
'There isn't anything that you can do.
Oh, you can give the child affection. Not too much,
Or else it marks her out from the other children.
You can't be a mother to them all,
And so you mustn't try to be to one,
Even supposing that you really could.'

There was a silence while they drank their tea.
Outside over redbrick lavatories
Marbled rain-clouds dragged and drifted by.
'Of course, I'm still getting to know the class,
And yet I think I'd noticed her before
As having the kind of look that no child should have.
I do believe her face will haunt me now.'

Coming in, the headmaster overheard her.
'I don't know who you're talking about,' he said,
'But whoever it is, if you're going to take to heart
The troubles of every child you ever teach
You'll never live past thirty.'
                    'This one's different.'
'Oh, they're all different', he said.
Except there's never anything one can do.'
He sat across the corner of a table,
Looking out of the window over the playground,
Talking above the vague din.
                    'Take your class alone.
Eddie, as you've probably noticed, smells.
None of the other children want to get near him.
At the Christmas party they were playing Bigamy –
You know, this game where two girls choose one boy –
'Isn't this fun,' said Eddie. I heard him say it.
The others all got partners. He was left
Looking round, in the middle of the floor,
Wondering why no one came to him.
He's stupid, but he's not quite stupid enough.
He realised, and didn't understand.

So much for Eddie. Anne's from a broken home,
Lives with the father, a long distance lorry driver.
Came into school one morning very white.
Said that her arm was hurting. She'd broken it
The night before. The father was away.

She's only eight, she didn't know what to do,
Just lay there all night. Then there's Janey West.
Mother's a tart, all mascara and furs.
Hasn't much time for Janey, either way.

That kid's crying out for affection. Rosemary here,
She'll tell you how when she first had her in the class,
And took some notice of her, praised her reading,
The child hung round her all term, holding her hand,
Gazing up. It got so she had to be hard.
There's twenty-nine other children in the class.

Jimmy. You won't like Jimmy. Nobody does.
His father knocks him about. He pinches things.
He was brought to me once. He screamed like an animal,
Afraid I was going to hit him. And Peter Blair.
He came in once, showed me a photograph.
'Who's that, Peter?' 'That's my Daddy', he said.
I knew his father. He left home when Peter was two.
'It's not now, is it, Peter?' 'Well, it's my uncle.'
'Why did you tell me it was your daddy then?'
'I thought perhaps my uncle was my daddy', he said.

Oh, I could go through half of them like that.
Annil Aktar. Annil's an immigrant.
Nice little chap when he came here. Great dark eyes.
The other kids call him Pakistani pest.
No need to ask where they get it. Of course, he reacts.
He can understand the tone if not the language.
He's turning vicious, sullen. Doesn't mix.
Let's face it. Half of these kids'll grow up delinquents.
What can we do? Is it our job to give them love?'

Outside the bell went for the end of break.
He slid off the table abruptly and dusted his hands.

The Nestlings

This is the time of year one finds the nestlings
Fallen, lying on concrete path or lawn,
With the long pink legs trailed backwards, and the wings
Fledgeless, merest blotches of purple and fawn
On the flesh-pale sides. The heads are folded back
On the thin bent necks, the eyes
Open but never blinking at the black
Ballet of ants, the fumblings of the flies.

I have found them sometimes far from roof or tree
And wondered how they came there, whether thieved
By predator or left deliberately
By foodless parents. Being half-relieved
To find them dead, I try at least to fulfil
Some rite, as a child does, making each its hole
But troubling no more with crosses, and ignorant still
Of any fit prayer for the uncertain soul.

Estate

Bulldozers draw the last stumps from the mud's slack mouth.
Some workmen in a group are mixing concrete
In a yellow mixer. I stand and watch grey sky
Come up above this edge-of-town estate,

Come up above scaffolded roofs and rain-pocked gardens,
The world revolving on a desolate axis
Of mud and broken bricks. What was conceived
Now quickens imperceptibly. From this

Yellow-pooled waste of clay, these tin tea-huts,
These piles of brick and lengths of mottled pipe,
Rags and linoleum and clumps of grass,
All that makes up this barren-seeming landscape,

The bricks shall slowly climb, themselves a stark,
Skeletal, unsentimental birth,
Waiting to be fleshed with all time brings
Between the sky's drift and the turning earth.

Think of that fruition, of that fleshing.
Think of the couples, mortgaging their lives
To debt and to each other, coming here.
Think of the wives,

Hanging out washing, talking over the fences,
Grown pregnant, leaning on the sink and staring
Past the back gardens to the woods,
Dreaming of spring.

Think of a thousand children, going to school
On a thousand mornings, enduring a million lessons,
Learning how to be bored, and how to enjoy
What boredom leaves. Think of the seasons,

Coming and going, bringing all kinds of weather,
But never so many days of sun or rain
As days like this, unmemorable, grey,
Yet with the rest not to return again.

And here will settle all the sediments
That peace permits: custom and occupation,
Those quicksands slowly swallowing our lives,
That nonetheless we take as their foundation.

And here will come the T.V. aerials,
Cars in the driveway, numbers on the gates,
Roses and chrysanthemums sharing front gardens
With stucco dwarf and dinghy – all that dates

An era afterwards, that gives its poignancy
Where nothing else – and what else will there be?
Beneath this shallowness, perhaps no deeper,
The acting out of a humanity.

For doors will be knocked, and what comes
Will never be quite what was expected or desired,
And some will die lonely in a darkened room,
Or live in one afraid.

And always there will be the sense of time,
The filling past, the lessening to be,
The sandgrains slipping through the narrow neck
Down into memory.

But here at least will be for some the place
That always they return to after absence,
The sacred ground on which are acted out
All the rituals of innocence.

And though to that sealed over earth no spring
Shall bring the blossoming of flower and tree
Still the blind sap shall not be denied
Its endless thrusting continuity,

As under this grey sky and in this time
The dumb assertion that will not despair
Begins again: trembling to be articulate
A rafter sways, then settles and is there.

Starlings

My father got up determinedly that Sunday.
'Those starlings had their boots on again last night.
I'll have to clear them out before they lay.'
I did not approve. But then I did not sleep in the room
On top of which they kept up such a brawling
And such a loving, in the dawn's small hours.

He poked a ladder up through the loft and climbed,
Descending some time later with a pailful
Of straw and mud, mixed with a few soft feathers.
('Breast feathers', I said), the remnants of four nests,
And threw them in the hedge. And I suppose
He could not do much else; but later on
You should have heard the clamour as those starlings
Came crying desolate about the eaves,
Stirring us each with some uneasiness,
Their wings above the windows beating at
The closed doors of our pity or our guilt,
Like old wrongdoings, coming home to roost.

Love after the Fall

Dwellers in a chalk and limestone country,
We never knew the well-watered valleys of Eden,
Whose Four Streams never ran dry,
The freshets and the fountains of that garden.

For long, it is said, we wandered in the desert
Where all the streams ran darkening into sand.
For survival, we sucked the damp grit
And in the dry storms held each other's hand.

Faithful we may have been, yet had no faith
To smite the living granite with a staff.
We were not the kind for miracles.
It was enough sometimes to hear you laugh.

And now we have come to our own territory,
No Eden, but the pastureland is good.
The waters flow here unpredictably,
But here at least is neither sand nor flood.

And we, the fallen lovers, knowing thirst,
Learned long ago to play the waiting part,
And have most joy in knowing after cloudburst
The winterbournes and swallets of the heart.

The Bonfire

And by the 4th, the bonfire was quite ready,
The central pole sunk in a four-foot pit
And wedged with flints; against its upper forks
Eight other saplings propped; these held secure
By interwoven crossboughs; finally,
Brushwood stuck in every interstice
And the hollow centre, that had been a camp
Where five could sit, or two hold against three
In clod and apple warfare, filled with boxes,
Paper, straw, a mattress and old boots.

On the next day only dew fell, damping
Nothing but the long grass in the fields
And after tea they all came out, the infants
Owl-eyed at the dark, the older children
Laughing and throwing bangers, but he the lictor
Bearing the torch of flaming tarry rag
Up through the smoky apple-smelling darkness,
Along the hedge, across the open field,
Under the wood's flint-dark and ferny leaf,
Till in the clearing where the bonfire was
They settled round him in a watching circle.

And he thrust the torch in low down through the side,
And in the woven darkness something stirred,
A glimmer, then a glow. He held it there
Till the whole structure grew alive with flame,
That licked along the interlacing twigs,
Became a sheet, hissed in the sappy evergreen,
Crackled up the dead leaves' fragile bronze,
And a gust of orange sparks whirled out and danced
Away beyond the trees. Then he stood back,
And the whole clearing sighed, and came to life.

There in the outer circle of the firelight
Dark figures moving in fantastic wreaths
Of green and ochreous smoke, fumbled with bottles,
Struck matches, hammered nails, or simply stood
In the leaping flamelight, wholly radiant,
Watching the dark-eyed, red-rimmed catherine wheels
Slow to a halt from their brief spinning brightness,
The rockets, quaking out in coloured stars,
That wandering lit up the whole night landscape,
And the Roman candles, and the fiery spinners,
The flowering trees of silver sparks, or just
The flames themselves, reflected on the oak trunks
Or blanching on one side the clumps of grass
That on the other cast long shadow-cones.

But scorched and smoke-grimed, he saw none of this.
The fire possessed him wholly and was perfect,
Still retaining that tight outer structure
But all its inside burning in one blaze,
So that the boughs stood out like mullions
And transoms of a window, that one looked through
Into some realm where like a salamander
Truth moving in a furious bright ardour
Transfigured everything. He stood entranced,
Seeing an old boot blister in the heat,
Its tongue on fire and curling up; each eyelet
Glowing separately. And cypress burned,
Dropping wire-white flakes of ash, yet keeping
Its shape so long, a bush of fire, pure fire,
Till almost he would not have been surprised
To understand its hoarse and roaring tongue.

And to do that, he would have done anything,
Or anything just to have kept it going,
Short, that is, of throwing on himself
(Though even that darted across his mind)
Or others. Even so, he did his best,
Gathering leaves and twigs and clumps of grass,

Sprinkling them in a kind of benediction,
Knowing at least that it was little more.
And the flames sank low. He saw them idly
Reading the pages of an open book
He raked up from the outskirts, that before
They would have swallowed in a fiery instant.
Now they only blackened, line by line,
The type still standing for a moment, silver,
Then crumbling. And he saw a fallen crossbough,
On top still burning with a braid of fire,
But bearded with white ash beneath, and then
For the first time, felt the darkness near
Over his shoulder, looking at the flames.

And the last rocket stitched the dark with stars.
The fire sank to a bed of glowing coals,
That still the light wind drew sometimes to brightness
But could not keep from going out, and now
Only the centre pole was left still upright,
Like a tall totem, half-charred through,
But ready to come down at any moment.
Seeing this, he stooped and seizing up
A burnt log from the outskirts of the fire
Slung it low and sideways at the pole,
Which broke. Slowly it toppled, swinging out
Its bright arc, and it seemed the brighter then,
The motion turning spark to glow, and glow
Might have become flame, but it hit the ground,
Though in such starry ruin that the night
Skittered back wildly to the clearing's edge.
Then the flames died, and the shadows died.

Even then he might have stood, but rain
Finished the thing off, hissing in the ash,
And coming out of dream he found himself
Cold, the others gone, and knew that now
There was nothing left for him to do but join them,
Out in the dark fields, looking in the grass
For burnt out cases and spent rocket sticks.

ABSENCES and CELEBRATIONS
1982

Returning after Absence

Returning after absence
We were aware of strangeness
    In the half-dark room,
As if we had come early
Somehow, and chanced to see
    Time in its act of custom
Altering our lives.
These shapes we knew, that held us,
    Seemed as strange as starlight
Queered by far galaxies.
We stood there, scared by shadows
    Of a coming summer night.
I turned to look at you
And at the same time you turned too,
    Each thinking: was the other changed?
One unfamiliarity
Shaking our long close-joined reality:
    I saw you time-estranged
As time will have us, even that loved face
Grown indistinct within a shadowed place,
    Until we touched, and laughed, and knew once more
That we were haunted, but not haunters yet
With time ahead of us to pay time's debt,
    And you put on the lights, and shut the door.

Not to be Born

No different, I said, from rat's or chicken's,
That ten-week protoplasmic blob. But you
Cried as if you knew all that was nonsense
And knew that I did, too.

Well, I had to say something. And there
Seemed so little anyone could say.
That life had been in women's wombs before
And gone away?

This was our life. And yet, when the dead
Are mourned a little, then become unreal,
How shall the never born be long remembered?
So this in time will heal

Though now I cannot comfort. As I go
The doctor reassures: 'Straightforward case.
You'll find, of course, it leaves her rather low.'
Something is gone from your face.

Father

Your coughing hurts me more. On winter mornings
And coming up the road it is your sign.
I see at last that you are growing old.
This summer you retired. Whose life with mine
Was mingled for so long and never noticed
More than as the flavour of a coat
Smelling of tobacco, as a forehead
Frowning at the desk-top where you wrote
Figures in a black book, adding up
To everything, to nothing, to a wage –
I whose youth so took your love for granted,
What answer can I make now to your age?

Father, it is too late. I want for you
All the chances that were never yours,
Summer . . . but what can come? Only the summer
That autumn brings, the days warm for five hours
After the mist clears, and before the sunset.
Father, then I want for you no less.
Here in the autumn garden where you sit
Unlearning slowly an old restlessness,
Red admirals still tremble on the stonecrop
And swallows come, as to a meeting place.
Read now, remember, watch your children's children,
And fall asleep with sunlight on your face.

Newborn

Welcome, my defeat,
Soft as a fall into snow,
My most gentle undoing.
Your hands reach up to me
With innocent gravity
Drawing me into love.
I must enter the circle of cooing
And nest with the dove.

The violent and the swift
Break on you, soft rock.
Love reefs you round.
Now I must leave the ocean
For this one lake devotion.
Ah, sweet man,
My son, my calm encircled ground,
Today I too began.

Mother

I saw you in the small room stooped above
The figure in the cot, to tuck or kiss,
Your face made soft by lamplight and new love,
And you complete now, in your mother's bliss,
    Calling him honey, and rose,

But tired, never now to be quite careless,
And learning what love asks, and how life goes,
Custodian of a consuming brightness,
The old moon's shadow, as the new moon grows.

Taxonomical Note

Not just the sizes named (like miniatures,
Littles, queens, King Kongs, dwarf alleys, alleys),
But patterns, lovingly. Like silvers, clears,
Coca-colas, bottle-washers, genies,

Sparkle alleys, squids ('thick squirmy patterns'
Says my six-year-old), propellers, maypole
Alleys ('sort of stripy'), spiderwebs
And snowflake alleys ('they're most beautiful').

I tell you, there's a poet in this country.
He is probably eight years old. His head is full
Of coloured glass and words. He is a maker,
Unread, untutored, immemorial.

Cool Medium

In fifty-three the children up our road
Got television and disappeared indoors
After school, instead of coming out
To toast crusts over stick fires in the hedgerow
Or fill the first-starred, batwinged dusks of autumn
With clamour of wild games. I sulked around

The silent woods, refused their invitations,
And hated ever since those moon-grey flickers
From a dead planet. Now, at night, I still
Walk past curtained windows, knowing each
Conceals that strange communion. Is life
Something to be given up for that?

Amused, superior, adult faces smile:
The awkward child stalks in the woodland still,
Keeping the ward of long-abandoned places,
As if one day the others might come back,
Stubborn in an antique heresy,
With trees and winter stars for company.

In Memory of Edward Thomas, 1878 – 1917

Between your pages so much lost was found
It seems a grief, that so much found is lost
To us who came too late and never now
Can walk with you and listen, as once Frost
Those summer nights. We see you ringed around,
As in the Malvern dusk, with friendship's rainbow
Who never dreamed that you would haunt us so.
Inheritors, we mourn your lucid image,
Lost in the dark indifference of our age.

And yet, those pages say, you were as much
Alone, we are always alone, it is always dark.
Your days were measured by the willow leaf
And by the restless unreturning brook.
Lonely, you feared the salt demanding touch
Of others' love; night brought for all relief
The aspen tree's unreasonable grief.
Only one thing you asked for in the end:
That language should blow through you like a wind.

Now, on an April evening, I read you again
And hear your voice survive its vanished past.
I think of how my heart, at first encounter,
Leapt to you like a needle, homing at last
On its north, yet in your lines the rules are plain:
Be wary. Walk alone. Watch, and endure.
One remedy for all regrets is sure ...
A winter grief that quickened long ago.
Tonight I listen and the spring winds blow.

Appeals

Almost daily the world
Bleeds through my letter-box. On the mat each morning
I find fresh gouts: blind babies, orphans, spastics,
The deaf, the lonely old, ill-treated pets,
Blue whales, otters, donkeys... Donkeys? Well,
Why not; in indiscriminate despair
I scribble out the breakfast cheques, each careful
Conscience-minimum. Now world, will you
Leave me alone today? Will someone else
Apply these scraps of dressing? But the blood
Seeps through, it stains my fingers, sometimes at night
Becomes a bright unlaunderable flood.
Can't someone tell them I've a life to lead?
Just so, they murmur, drawing off, and bleed.

Water Music

Here at the corner of the rock where sun
Silvers the wet rocks as the ripple leaves them,
In among the rocks and all around them
Soft bells of water sound a constant canon
Even in the calmest summer air –
The music of not going anywhere
That quiet water makes against the land.

Today we have come far among the rocks
Looking for coloured stones and bits of shell,
Hearing the lift and sigh of the long swell
Diminuendo down a thousand cracks.
Green water and a glow of amber stone,
The sun still burning, not much past the noon,
And music rippling all around my hand.

FLINTS
1986

Flints

We walk on whiteness, inches under grass.
Few would call it rock: these infant hills
Brittle as the bones of cuttlefish,
Will never last, they'll flow away like milk
In the next great rain and stain the tide,
And something will be left.
                   We dug a soak-pit,
Chambering the chalk, a well of white
Four foot deep and every bite the spade
Took of that smooth cake the tooth would jar
On something we must pry out: one more stuck
Flour-covered fruit-stone. There they lie, loose-piled,
Just as they'll lie a million years from now
Rubbling some scoured valley. Now my hands
That fought them loose fit lovingly around,
I feel for heft and socket-hollow, thumb
A sleek black shining.
                   Look, a tribe of dour
Dark-skinned aboriginals. They wait
Through bland white epochs, thick-skulled, underground.

At the Open-air Market

The long-haired huckster fans a stack of plates:
One pouring shuffle, like a waterfall.
Smells of crushed grass, frying onions, crates.
A crowd like driftwood builds against his stall.

Housewives mostly, ready for a lark.
He gets them going with a tale or two
Then settles to it, looking for a mark.
Beneath the smile his eyes appraise: And you?

Relax, friend. I'm not here to cramp your style.
Purveyors, like consumers, have their rights.
On with the foxy patter: I may smile
But only at a memory that lights

My mind up suddenly, like sun through mist,
Of how you once stole linen from a hedge
In palmy days when young wives could be kissed
Before life set your pugging tooth on edge,

And at another time how plausibly
With what aplomb you preached as you bestowed
Pigs' bones and pardons round the company
In April on the Canterbury road.

Harvest

The field that started where my garden ended
Grew wheat and spring was green, a ribboned rustle
That silvered to the wind. But it was summer
We waited for: to rise in some blue dawn
And find the harvest started; on the hill
The cutter's wake of windrows, blond and glinting
Till baled and stacked they stood again in gold.

Shy as mice, we children watched from hedges
Until the workers went, then out we came
To battle on the slope with stubble-bombs
Or lug the bales to build, like chambered barrows,
Roofed passages where in the ripe hot dark
We sat exchanging stores, intimate,
Remoter from the world than Timbuctoo.

Did seasons last so long in that brown land?
We thought those harvest days would never end
And when they did there was another morning.
Yet autumn came: the wild green clematis
Turned to snow and coal-dust on the hedges,
The jigsaw pattern of the sunbaked paths
Melted, and the paths led out of summer.

Once though, my father took me where the men
Were working in the great barn, stacking up.
I watched them in the sunshot, moted darkness
And thought it then so fine a thing; there was
No play I would not trade to be as these
With salt-stung hands, sharing the harvest honour,
Least of, but known among, that company.

The Computer Room, Midnight

The air's cave-chill. You need two coats in here.
No seasons, nothing varies. Day and night
Walls hum, the white-tiled ceiling casts its light
On racked arrays; all's shadowless and clear.
For here's a place of clarity. And I
Inhabit it; secure I move between
These ordered oracles: see at this screen
I pause with midnight-hollowed eyes to scry:
At once the legend answering appears
Lettered in green fire: initiate,
I understand these matters; I dictate,
The strange beasts purr, obey me. Fifteen years
Of mastering these beautiful unmeanings,
Neat as a titmouse building nests of logic,
Conditioned by reward to run rat-slick
Down these electric mazed meanderings.
Time to go home. I sign the exit page,
Wish the guard good-night. Outside the dark
Is wild: great clouds rise up, a ragged murk
Obliterates the moon's faint silver rage.
I walk the empty roadways, I surrender
To masterless complexities of wind.
Back inside, the snowflakes of my mind
Are melting on the black boots of the future.

Small Incident in Library

The little girl is lost among the books.
Two years old maybe, in bobble cap,
White lacy tights, red coat. She stands and looks.
'Can't see you, Mummy.' Mummy, next row up,
Intent on reading answers absently:
'I'm here, love.' Child calls out again: 'Can't see.'

A large man, his intentions of the best,
Stoops: 'Where's Mummy, then?' Child backs away.
Now the tall shelves threaten like a forest.
She toddles fast between them, starts to cry,
Takes the next aisle down and as her mother
Rounds one end disappears behind the other.

I catch the woman's tired-eyed prettiness.
We smile, shake heads. The child comes back in sight,
Hurtles to her laughing, hugs her knees:
'Found you!' in such ringing pure delight
It fills the room, there's no one left who's reading.
The mother looks down, blinking. 'Great soft thing.'

Frogs

Blob on the lawn.
Black elastic flicker.
Blob on the path and the frogs are back, moving to spawn
In the spring night, travelling
By roads they remember.

Crouched in the dark,
Watching each quick soft rise,
I see in a garden long gone a child stooped to mark
Something unknown, not moving:
A yellow stone with eyes.

Strangeness, delight.
The lost world summons, near,
Softly electric, returning in leaps from the night,
My root-kin, my renewing,
At the spring of the year.

Yobs

Me in the rain, my scooter broken down,
Fed up, pushing it, and these four lads
Block the pathway, jeering. Now, why's that?
No idea: for sure they don't know me.
I know them though (villages have eyes):
Petty vandals, go round daubing walls,
Snap the aerials off cars at night,
Wreck the children's playground, damage trees,
Tear the flowers up. Oh, I know them,
Know who's been expelled, in court. I know
Other things: I know who's unemployed,
Who come from broken homes, whose mother went,
Dumped him, four years old, to live with Gran,
I know who loiter now, unreachable,
By wasteland in the rainy winter dusk,
Who cry out 'Look at us!'
                              Not my affair.
I stand then, blocked, aggression's logan-stone
Poised, exquisite.
                        So, who's leader? You,
Tall, in leather jacket, skull-adorned.
'Afternoon. You any good with these?
My baffle-pipe's gunged up, I've sheared the screw.'
Silence. Jacket boy considers me.
Thinking what? We've got a right one here?
Puzzled? Wary? I don't know. And then
'Hey, look, what you do...' 'He needs...' 'No, look...'
Hands in concert, octopoidal, blurring,
Strip, clean out, refit. I clear my throat,
Fumble in my pocket, find two pounds.
'Look, I'd like...' The leader, kneeling still,
Wipes his oily fingers, straightening,
Hesitates, then smiles and shakes his head.
The scooter starts first time. I ride away.

The Visit

Ahead, the others talked
   When the bus had set us down.
Four foot tall I walked
   The unfamiliar town,

And voices in my head
   Were speaking, grave and clever:
If the known should die, they said,
   The world will change forever.

That day of blaze and shade
   The tarry crooked street
Where once my father played
   Stood empty in the heat.

The terraced house was narrow,
   The stairs were dark and steep
Where children long ago
   Went candlelit to sleep.

Stifled in their cases
   The books inhaled again.
The photographs' dry faces
   Drank up my youth like rain.

And round and round the table
   Above the covert ears
The voices like a fable
   Were sighing for the years.

They might have saved their sighing.
   For all their child's endeavour
The known has died, is dying.
   The world is changed forever.

Postcard from Pembrokeshire

My friends, who go so lightly here and there,
Who jet-propelled, car-catapulted view
Lands, cities, histories and never care
That none of it is yours or speaks to you,
I know you'd laugh to see me here perplexed
Still after two weeks by the rocks and seas
Of one domestic unfamiliar text
Missing my rooted etymologies
Of Chiltern beech. Yet there's no other way
For us, the slow ones, who would understand
The language of the summer clouds that lay
Their shivering allusions on the land.
We grow like lichen outwards, take an hour
To gloss the gannet's sky-and-ocean glide
Or lost in lexicons of tree and flower
Will walk daylong, while by the waterside
The dancing runes of river-light on slate
All but reveal the lost . . . And summer ends
Before one sentence of it's learnt. Too late,
And yet today, out round the green bird islands
Where seagulls dipped to meet their soaring shadows
On sunlit cliff, it seemed to me I heard
Some phrase, one morning fragment . . . Well, who knows?
I send my love, I'll keep that summer word.

The House Martins

The night we quarrelled I went down to the beach
And twenty martins were there, weaving their flight
Under the sandstone cliffs in the last of the light.
Each had its own niche-moulded nest and each
Would leave in turn to twinkle, skim and dive
Then come like bees re-entering a hive
To hang in folded stillness. It became
Like a compulsion, counting each one back
To fit them in mosaic, white and black
Against the glowing cliff, or like that game
One plays with balls, for as the last flew in
So all the rest would tumble out and spin
In wider circles on the twilit sea.
Nothing I could do would stop that flight
Or lodge the last one in its nest till night
Called the birds back and brought them silently
To rest once more beneath the old scarred rock
That wind and wave had made a butcher's block.

Meetings

Sometimes behind the words of those you meet
You come upon a lost unshareable
Hinterland: some slate-roofed town, mediaeval
In morning light, a dalehead where they walked
Between moss-felted walls... it's there so plain
You step like deer into this new terrain
Until you feel them falter, having talked
Some moments to you gone, so you return
From that deep journey back to surfaces
Yet ever after taste their lives like loss.
How can you tell them this? Unless, in turn,
You meet sometimes another watching too
Behind the words unshareable lost you.

Say

Say that you're at work, and that it's summer.
July. The swifts cry out above the street.
Blinds are drawn against the light-dazed city.
    The office dreams in heat.

Say that there's a quiet dark-haired woman,
(Days like this, a man might fall in love),
With her wide quick smile to walk with you and sit
    At lunch with leaves above.

Say you talk together, oh, of nothing –
Dogs, yoghourt, husbands, children, wives,
Just the way we do that confidential
    Casual trade of lives.

Say you know, for all a million reasons,
Nothing is between you, nor could be,
That she is young, not even to remember
    The hour, your company.

Say you know it, but this day of summer
Touches you as soft as summer rain.
Light, leaves, her green and hazel eyes
    Work in you deep like pain.

Say, returning home, you sit that evening
At twilight under blossom on the grass,
Talking with your wife about your children
    The way such evenings pass.

Say that clarity returns, with laughter
For foolish love, but under it despair.
Say you know it now, that pain of sunlight:
    Your youth gone, hard to bear.

Blooding

Coming back in late September twilight
After a good day out, the children singing,
A full moon yellow in the east and sunset
Dulling in the west above the cornfields,
We came on something in the quiet road:
A hare, run over, left to die, back legs
Smashed quite flat: a stuck moth, fluttering,
And yet not dead, but panicking wild-eyed,
Arching in the dazzle, pushing up
On boxer's shoulders, falling, pushing up.
No one spoke. My children looked and waited
Me? What competence had I in death?
I started off to let the car roll forward,
All set to do it in the modern way,
A filthy casual obliteration,
And could not: took a spanner and knelt down
Saying words. The great eyes rolled, went quiet.
I lifted it, the body cold as dew
Before I even laid it in the bracken.
No more singing. At the door my wife
Met us: 'What on earth . . .' My little one:
'Daddy couldn't help it', ran upstairs.

Squirrel

Squirrel, like a blob of mercury,
Spills intact through cataracts of tree.

Squirrel's all but bird to nest and fly,
Walks on thin black twigs like cracks in sky.

Squirrel is half tail, a wave of smoke,
A plume, a catkin; squirrel's lord of oak

And walks the copse, not caring if he's seen.
Be prudent, squirrel, keep the trunk between,

But if you must forget, then be as now:
A woodland gargoyle, watching from the bough

As if to ask, 'What does it want of me,
That strange, untrustable, two-legged tree?'

A Local History

Digging in his garden, someone found
A Celtic head, green-skinned, with faint smooth hair,
The nose fine-chiselled still, and beautiful
   The falcon stare.

North's the Roman road, but long before
The Ridgeway crossed these hills, oldest of lanes.
Blue cloaks, mud-spattered, gold-torqued warriors.
   The mud remains.

At Englefield the warboats of the Vikings
Startled the herons from their reedy bed.
Alfred attacked, drew back; the cold green river
   Received the dead.

Stephen and Matilda: Wallingford.
The winter land cried out for God's relief.
In the beechwoood's grey cathedral trees
   Put forth new leaf.

King Charles's men, by secret furzy ways
Came south by here to fighting in the town.
Richard Atkyns mourned his men 'like fruit
   The wind blows down'.

Records for last century: one winter
Five babies dead, winds cold, much frost again.
Water from the ponds, mud floors, the roads
   Milky with rain.

Beside the recreation ground a cross:
There died so many, from so small a place.
Still among the old a few remember
   A name, a face.

Nineteen eighty. New estates, new people,
The easeful lives of rootless liberty,
While the stone head watches, and the woods
   Wait silently.

Gaia's Dream

Even now, there are places that remember.
Here, where the rocks are rounded to the north
And sleek as seals from that old polishing,
Where valleys end mid-air, sawn-off, and lakes
Sudden in the hollows under crags,
Flash like kingfishers, the earth will dream.
They come back then. A million blue-white snails
Rasping their way with boulder-studded tongues...
Their licks and furrowings disturb her: see,
She shivers in her sleep, the sun has gone,
The wind is from the peak, the lake's still eye
All pupil now stares inwards, black, opaque.
Ten thousand years are buried in that blink.
And where are we? Diminished, back to scale,
A scattered few, precarious in caves,
Enduring at the edges of her dream.
Again she cradles us with cruel love:
Her latest kind, whom she might come to favour
Or else, tomorrow, might scour off for good.

The Haunted Road

That was the route I loved best
In all my running: a road
Hollow between high banks
Where the farm carts took their load.
The moons of after-harvest
Shone on the dust and showed
Embossed each glinting grain.
The haystack's reek in winter
Was summer's breath again.

That road was haunted, they said:
A tall dark man would glide
Out of the shadows and move
Keeping pace at your side.
A hood would be over his head,
If you spoke he never replied
Till looking down you would see
Whatever walked beside you
Ended at the knee.

No ghosts kept this boy back,
Not then, though the hairs of the young
Rose in the pitch-dark hollows
That the hedges overhung.
So now, shall I fear the track
Or those I walk among,
Though keeping pace they glide:
My escort of the shadows,
The dark man at my side?

Not Daffodils

Less pleasant now, to lie,
Half-dreaming, half-awake,
And watch with inward eye
The images that break.

Not daffodils, my love,
But falcons of remorse
Attend me from above
And track my desert course,

Or water rises fast,
A dark and closing sea,
Where present joins to past
In salt complexity,

Or else that fire, once out,
New-kindled in my brain,
A winter wind of doubt
Extinguishes again.

Air, water, fire: which leaves
Another element.
That image also grieves
And is not heaven-sent.

My love, I hear you claim
It's what you've always said:
That small good ever came
From idling on a bed.

Come then, and exorcise
My vacant, pensive mood
With your clear outward eyes.
People my solitude.

Another Small Incident

November evening, rain outside and dark
Beyond the building's honeycomb of warmth.
The old man stands there, waiting to be noticed.
He wears propitiation like a coat.
The girl looks up at him. 'Yes? Can I help?'
'This card you sent like, that's the problem, see.
It says I've got your book, but that's not right.
I mean, I had it but I brought it back.
That's what I do, I read one, bring it back.
I never keep them, see.'
                              He stands, condemned
Yet quivering for justice. 'All right, sir.'
She smiles at him. 'We get mistakes like that.
Just leave the card with me.' He stares at her,
Seventy, with spotted hands, afraid,
And someone smiles at him and calls him sir.
Lighting at the contact, like a bulb,
He warms to her. 'That's what I do, you see.
I take the one, I read it, bring it back.
I thought, you know, it might be on the shelves.
I mean, if no one's had it since like, see?'
Another girl comes by. 'We're closing , Sue.
You coming?' Sue looks up and rolls her eyes.
The old man catches it. He understands.
He turns and shuffles out into the night.

Outskirts

Someone should speak of these peculiar margins,
Neither town nor country, where nobody goes.
The cornfields seems abandoned, yet corn grows.
The pasture's shaggy, like a firing-range.
Who cares for this, who keeps it? One begins
To wonder sometimes. I have stood at twilight
Watching swifts around an empty grange,
Black boomerangs, returning in their flight
So close their wings have clipped me. There's a fear
About this. Where has everybody gone?
Almost comforting the ridged horizon
Contains the motorway's lit pouring sea.
Even so, I do not go too near.
It would not to risk a certain sight,
No traffic there but wind, and endlessly
The shining pistils stretching into night.

Dune Country

Crouched, I become the land
Flexing its lion shoulders. The light torments me.
Something's far out, it dazzles on the sea.
　The wind comes, driving sand
Minute by minute, bearing my substance away.
How shall I root and stay?

　I stand my shifting ground.
I build defences, knit with marram, heal with moss.
The sift, the scurry, whisperings of loss
　Continue all around.
These brambles with their blood-dark leaves, their fruits are
　　　　　　　　　　　　　　　　　　　mine.
They taste of mud and brine.

　Gulls glitter in the height.
Men, when they come, are the odd ones, walking alone.
The sea brings driftwood, delicate as bone.
　I drum to gales of light.
Wind tears my roots, throws down my building, all's in vain.
I lie low, try again.

October Fungi

They are back again, the people of the woods,
A travelling circus of freaks: they have pitched their camp
On meadows of moss between the boles of beeches.
There's no concealment here: they loll on stumps
In sulphur tribes or swagger in the leaves
Scarlet as outlaws. Fear is in their names:
Destroying Angel, Deathcap, Sickener.
The darkness bred them, devilry's their lore
And parody their style. There's Dryad's Saddle
Perched, a monstrous butterfly of leather;
This velvet sleek translucence is Jew's Ear,
There's blewit's ghostly lilac, polypores
Rubber-tough or textured like meringue,
Smelling of peach and honey. So we meet
Towards another year's end in the woods.
What shall I say to you, gay-sinister
Consorts of corruption? Welcome, life.
The slugs have gorged themselves on stinkhorn jelly
And here's a puffball ready to explode,
A wrinkled cerebellum, parchment-yellow,
A rotted sack of flour that splits and spills.
The spores rise up, dream-delicate, like smoke.
They glint and dwindle down the shining air.

Anniversary

A rapids-rider, finding this brief stay,
No more perhaps than where the waters gather
In amber calm before the next cascade,
I turn and see, surprised at my surprise,
(Unthinkable it could be otherwise)
That you're here too: have threaded your own way,
So close yet separate, by shoot and boulder
Through the daze and din of time's white water.

You smile again with that old innocence.
I think: the springs of youth did not foretell
These cataracts... I dreamed you swan-like, made
To drift beneath green courtesies of willow,
Your cygnet brood unendingly in tow.
What brought you then to such a turbulence,
Time or I? Yet we are here; the swell
Draws our craft together. All is well.

Finders Keepers

All was to be revealed,
  Labelled and exact,
As on some site lies peeled
  Each layered artefact,

But memory, you prove
  No archaeologist
So patiently to move
  No crumb of life is missed.

The flashing random spade
  Ungovernably delves.
Who thought to see displayed
  Such debris of lost selves?

Stranger, should there glint
  Upon this ruined scene
Among the clay and flint
  Amazingly washed clean

Some relic, then receive
  If lost indeed be found,
The right of trove I leave
  To this my troubled ground.

SETTLEMENTS
1991

Map-maker

There ought to be a survey done, with maps.
One shouldn't come upon them unawares.
I mean the places where you fall through time.
You know them by a lifting of the hairs,
A sudden tense alertness, not quite fear,
The air's electric whisper: *who goes here?*

It happens anywhere: an old canal,
The corner of a field, a cobbled mews.
I'd plot them all, a pointillist of time.
I've worked it out, the colours that I'd use:
Vermilion for the present, shading back.
The past's autumnal spectra end in black.

My maps would be a handbook for the haunted.
There'd be blood-red, then, for the motorways
With cities in their web like scarlet spiders,
But over here, in delicate flint-greys,
High on the downs pure Neolithic time
In chalky hollows, lingering like rime.

For furthest back, before the glaciers,
I'd let sloe-purple paint the night of caves.
My Roman ghosts would rise in blues and ochres
And Bronze Age russet glint about old graves.
How lovingly I'd chart one valley's scene
In Saxon gold and fresh mediaeval green.

But there's no school for time's cartographers
And any skill of mine to mark and keep
I'd lavish on the contours of the living.
It's only sometimes, at the edge of sleep,
I watch imagined colours pulse and fade.
How beautiful, the maps I never made.

Scents

Tonight the rain in summer dark
Releases scents of leaf and bark:
The fumy reek of resined trees
And currant's sweet acridities.

Those aromatic compounds fit
Some membranous receptive pit
And trigger in my waiting brain
The memory of other rain.

I learnt my seasons from no class:
My summers were wild rose and grass,
A velveted and honeyed air.
Tonight I know: the past is there

And lies, so little does it need
To live again, in bush and weed
A yard or two beyond my door.
I am the child I was before.

Odours of earth, like love they came
Before the word, before the name.
The gates of time swing wide for these
Primaeval analeptic keys.

Then let me keep, though all depart,
These strange familiars from my start:
As in my first, in my last air,
Most potent molecules, be there.

Night

Night is another country, like the past.
   I study there,
Learning how small a light will do at last:
   A muffled moon, one star,
How puddles in the blackest winter night
   Will spread a blacker glimmer, how the frost
Will lantern leaf and twig with haloed light
   To guide the lost.

I've watched, a darker shadow from the shade,
   Five badgers pass
Like broken moonlight moving in the glade;
   I've come on deer at grass
And fled with them the blind assaults of cars
   Like flash-floods in the gully of the lane
And waited till the only light was stars
   And seen again.

The unlit land is in me: when the towns
   Are loud with day
I close my eyes: a night-wind from the downs
   Has cleared the mist away.
The god I make myself is deep and still,
   Absorbing all, an endless starry dark.
I hear the train far off behind the hill,
   The farm dogs bark.

For Beth

Dearest arrival, what a time to come.
Just when the party was over, never a doubt,
For children change, my love, they must go out
From the haven of our help, tall sons become
Voyagers: that's it, never again,
I thought, that trust, that sweet enquiring talk.
Families grow, like petals on a stalk.
Time is a wind that plucks. A gentle pain:
The years, I called it, nothing to regret.
We never thought, or dared, to ask for more,
Yet now you come, a small one, to our shore,
Time's compensation, our last gift and debt.
Sleep then, my daughter, on this guarded strand.
None ever came more welcome to my land.

Settlements

In those days you were always moving on
To the place that didn't need you, to the town
With its milling squares and grey aloof cathedral
Or the village where the memories went down
So deep the conversations of the old
Were roots of willow threading time's black mould.

And the places took no note of you, or smiled
Seeing you come, intent on reverence,
But then retired, to business or stillness,
Behind the stone facade, the pinewood fence.
Where can the young belong? What can they own?
You travelled onward, unaddressed, alone.

Yet sometimes you would stop beside the road
In a place that was no place at all, you'd say –
One shuttered shop, a forecourt hazed with petrol,
The heat and silence of a summer day –
And voices would be round you, conjuring
The gift of something you alone could bring.

Or on the upland maybe, in a field
Where history had never been at all
You'd stop to shelter from a burst of rain,
Crouched in the nettled angle of a wall,
And feel about you, like a beating heart,
The dispossessed, unwilling to depart.

And you would stop your ears, and turn away:
Was this the heritage for which you came,
The edge of things, the spare, the unobserved,
All that had lost, or never knew, its name?
Somewhere another kingdom lay in wait.
You hurried on towards your true estate.

You are older now. You have your own domain,
A narrow land, but country of your choice.
It blurs a little, known so long, so well,
But not the other. Clearer now the voice
Of all that sought you, heavier the debt
You cannot pay, or own to, or forget.

Widow

Twelve years alone. I watch time hunt you down.
Each meeting now, another earth is stopped:
Some building gone you knew from long ago,
Another friend to visit, lying propped
On death-ward pillows. What I do, I know –
The Sunday calls, the lunches in the town –
Weighs in the balance lighter than a leaf
Against the steady boulder of your grief.

I listen to the worries of the old:
The forms they send you, buses that don't run,
The closing shops, the tradesmen that won't call –
The genteel expectations one by one
Fall from your life. I listen to it all.
I counsel: have your comforts, don't get cold,
As if what tracked you were not sure and slow
And colder than a winterfull of snow.

Another place, another century
There might have been a solace for your kind:
The corner by the fire, the gathered children,
A life, to be recounted and refined.
They would have honoured you, that otherwhen:
Curator of the tribe, great mother-tree,
The rooted one with ripeness on her bough.
Your tribe is scattered: who will honour now?

We part. Again you tell me not to come
If roads are bad, if I've too much to do.
I reassure. I drive off in the dawn.
'You've got your job to get to.' Yes, that's true.
The pulpy silence of the winter lawn
Will start to beat within you like a drum.
I've left you something: cups to clear away.
You'll read the paper, wash up, face the day.

Place-Names

'The place-names all hazed over
With flowering grasses...'
Philip Larkin, *MCMXIV*

They are worn and durable
   As silvered oak,
The old names: Coombe and Barton,
   Stow and Stoke,

Burying the land
   Leaf-litter deep,
Gorgeous as Arundel
   Or plain as Steep.

Improbable on signs
   The past remains:
A Norman lorded here,
   There died the Danes.

That dyke the Saxons dug,
   This river-name
Murmured its light sound
   When Caesar came.

Bless the namers, men
   Of pen or plough.
History, receive
   Another now.

Poet, labourer,
   They do not pass.
We scent them on the map
   Like new-mown grass.

On The Motorway

Lonely on the motorway, the light
Fading fast and eighty miles to go,
I conjure ghosts to travel with tonight
And see you there, your cigarette aglow,
No different for fourteen years of death,
And neither of us wholly at our ease,
As if we went to speak, but held our breath,
The way it always was. At last, to please,
'Nice car' you say. I shrug, indifferent.
You know we've judged life otherwise again,
But now for once I see your good intent
And what it overlies, the hidden pain.
We never talked. I know you wanted to.
I drew my silent pentacle around.
It would have hurt too much to let love through.
Too late, I'd ask you in now to my ground.
'I never understood...' A silent touch.
The darkness turns. 'Was it like this for you:
That all you did seemed never to be much,
But what you did was all that you could do?'
You nod. 'I'm sorry.' 'Don't be. Children learn.
You think love's ever wasted?' Something bright.
The cigarette is gone, next time I turn.
I travel on, alone again, through night.

Relatively Speaking

If we could have time slower
   Our longing might arrest
And keep the lightning's flower
   Dendritic, silver, pressed
On night's black slate forever,
   But love is dispossessed.

If we could have time faster,
   Our knowledge by such speed
Might have the coming chapter
   And all time's book to read
Till starlight's tale is over,
   But time will pay no heed.

Since no art yet can alter
   That enigmatic rate,
Upon a steady river
   We travel, yet await,
And understand time's answer
   Too soon, or else too late.

Vocabularies

Like stars, or swarming bees, or flocks of birds,
We think them hardly countable, our words.

Yet fifty thousand's all we use, it seems,
For truth and lies, reality and dreams.

Which puzzles me. The world's more things than that.
Do languages grow lean as lives grow fat?

Is so much absent from our brains and eyes?
What's lost, I say, when we economize?

There's too much difference we make the same.
All poets love the miracle of name

Yet mourn exactitudes they cannot state:
The single noun that might denominate

Their moods of quietness like falling snow,
Or yearn for lexicons they cannot know:

The speech of eagles, what the dolphins sing,
The glossolalia of leaves in spring...

Nothing, we dream, could bring us to content
But fifty million words for what we meant,

To fit whatever happened like a glove,
Redeeming lost pluralities of love,

Until we wake to truth, and see again
Unharvested, like leagues of sunset grain,

Outnumbering all stars and bees and birds,
The matchless universe beyond our words.

The Maharajah's Well

I love this well, that stands among the trees,
Gorgeous-preposterous, like a bower-bird,
With its cupola of chocolate and gold
Topped by a burnished spike, like the twist of a turban,
With its shining elephants, and scroll of carp.

It was Ishree, Maharajah of Benares,
That wrote to Edward Reade, Lieutenant Governor,
Born in the Ipsden country, friend to Benares
Through years of famine and mutiny, missing always
A far-off hamlet lost among the beechwoods,

'Edward, that story you told me troubles me.
To think of a child being beaten for stealing water!'
(The melt of glaciers carved out our valleys;
Since then no stream's endured: the waters glug
And vanish through the fine white sieve of chalk).

'Ours is a dry land too. Let a well be sunk
For our friendship's sake, and the sake of your people at
home.'
And so it was done, in eighteen sixty three
By Wilder of Crowmarsh, a foot for each day of the year
Hand-dug through chalk and perilous shored-up gravel,

And the Maharajah paid, and Edward Reade
Bought land, appointed a keeper, raised an orchard,
And bonfires blazed in the Maharajah's honour
That none need trudge again, raw-handed with buckets,
To clay-lined ponds half-choked with weed and rush.

Now this is true: you can go and see for yourself,
Since virtue is always surprising, like an oasis,
For the Maharajah is dust on the thirsty plain
And Edward Reade came home and departed at last
Into the dry-leaved silence of the beechwoods,

And water was brought by pipe: the well was barred,
But the dome is there, by the road among the trees,
And the shaft remains: if they let a bucket down,
They could draw up water still from the aquifer,
It would tremble again in the light, it would quicken and
                                            quench.

Paths

What country has such paths? Our maps are green,
Reticulated like an insect's wing.
I love those veins. I trace them, summoning
Salt-road, flint-road, holloway: each scene
Rises responsive to my finger's course
As dot and dash pulse out their living morse.

These are the roads that talk. No tarmac here
To gag time's voice. That rut, that blue-rubbed stone,
Those polished roots say footsteps not my own
From immemorial kept my paths clear.
I see that long procession, race on race,
Moving before me at time's proper pace.

I'd follow it: look for me, if you will,
On some brown pathway like a spit of sand
That lakes of bluebell lap on either hand
Or on the green road where it mounts the hill,
The drover's road: I'd like to fall asleep
In wind and sunlight, counting vanished sheep.

But mostly under beeches look for me
Or listen where my rustling feet would cross
The paths that moonlight knows beneath the moss.
My shadow will be sharp... How can this be
Denied to me: was I not all my days
A woodlander and keeper of the ways?

Urban Grass

Last of the green companions, grass,
You stand at bay in nature's pass
With banners threadbare but unfurled
Against a steel and concrete world.

In strip and square, on dusty banks,
In trodden, flayed, polluted ranks,
On arid marl and burning clay
Your long resistance wears away.

What Sparta bred you, not to yield
One acre of the stricken field,
Though none lament, where you obeyed,
The stubborn, democratic blade?

Or does the wind bring news again
And is it told about the plain
In some ancestral singing home
Of fog and fescue, bent and brome?

I dreamed earth had its honour too
That lived, for all that we could do.
I walked saluting in the street
The armies that will not retreat.

Survivor

What's lost each century? The one before.
He's ninety. Quieter, he says. More green.
I glimpse it through him like a closing door.

He calls with things: a book, a magazine.
Can't stop, he says. Sits down, deplores the news,
Drinks coffee, talks of countries that he's seen.

Pressed trousers, overcoat, black shiny shoes.
He brings the children gifts: a joke, a sweet.
They listen to him but the clothes amuse.

How could they comprehend the long retreat:
But in good order, like a Guards' brigade,
Acknowledging withdrawal, not defeat,

Though all the roads run seaward? He has stayed
Too long he says, won't do; shakes hands; steps out
Stiffly; late, you'd think, for some parade.

Plural

It's birth begins it, our disunity:
From one to not-one, so we learn to count.
Fingered by the first mists of infinity
Two is a signpost where the numbers mount
Up past all eyried crags by Cantor's track
To what no mind can visit and come back.

Who was it though? What prophet, mage or king
Was first, the very first, to dare that land?
What thunders pealed, that day of reckoning
We took the integers from God's own hand,
That starry knowledge, heavier than stone,
And came down-mountain, plural and alone.

Against Geologies

Our seconds rain like shells of lime
To build great thicknesses of time:
We watch the secret moments fall
Anonymous beyond recall,
Since who will look for you and me
In those white beds of history?

But if they do, with prying pen
When all our now has turned to then,
Let them not think, because they find
Some particle we left behind,
They know the vanished sea above
That was our salt and sunlit love.

These words I leave for them to learn
Like lily's stem or print of fern
Are but our shadow in the stone
And all the rest is ours alone.
Then what a world of touch and talk
Shall lie compacted into chalk.

Hush-a-bye, Baby

All right, dear, I'll not risk bad dreams again
For our small daughter, singing her to sleep
With my sad ballads. Now Sir Patrick Spens
Can stay dry-shod; Queen Jane shall not cry out
For Good King Henry in her agony;
The channering worm shall chide no more; fair Janet
Must leave her true-love to the elf-queen's keeping,
And Arlen's wife will absolutely not
Be pinned right through the heart against the wall.
Henceforth, as you request, I shall confine myself,
Like any normal dad, to nursery rhymes:
Strange egg-shaped characters will smash themselves
Irreparably; ill-housed, harassed mothers
Whip hungry children; babies fall from trees;
Mice shall be maimed; sheep lost; arachnophobes
Fare badly; innocent domestics suffer
Sudden nasectomies, and at the end
We shall dance rosy-faced in a ring and drop dead with
                                         the plague.

In either case, outside the small lit bedroom
The glass shall weep with rain, the winds be howling
Their old, uncensorable savageries.
But you are right, of course: we should choose well
What songs we sing, to lull them for a while.

My People

My people never tell their love:
  Love ends where revelations start.
They keep it tethered like a yacht
  On private waters of the heart.
Some evening on the twilit roads
  They slip their moorings and depart.

That narrow craft each mans alone
  And none that watch those sails unfold
May know what skies are borne away
  Slow-gathered in the silent hold,
Nor if, upon another shore,
  Love makes a landfall, and is told.

Second Summer

That was the summer when you named the world.
I'd push you round the lanes or carry you,
Your small face eager, wanting to be told,
And me too anxious, sometimes, for your due:
I wanted so much for you, mountains, seas,
As if it weren't enough for anyone
What I could give: one village with its trees,
Its cooing doves, its verges hot with sun,
And all around it, fold on secret fold,
My watchful land, the silences of moss,
The meditations of an ancient loss.

What did I think imagination needs?
Were Edens never nondescript before
With tarry fence and yellow wayside weeds,
Or had I grown too tall for love's first door?
Ah, when I thought I took you by the hand
Who was it led the other one to see
By lane and bank the lost enchanted land
Forever in its wordless mystery,
And when you blew the clock of silver seeds
That says that time is always and the same
Which of us taught, which of us learned, the name?

The Beech Tree

Ten years ago I lay in hospital,
Not ready for it, tense, unsociable,
Stopped, as I had not been since I was born.
There was a tree: I'd wake to it each dawn,
All seethe and glimmer by my window pane,
And through the hot days turn and turn again
To where that house stood open: there were rooms,
Stairs, translucent attics, raftered glooms;
I'd lie beneath the lifting silken eaves
And feel the sunlight on my skin of leaves
And when I slept, within me I kept furled
The web and lattice of a secret world.
Not easy for my kind, the stubborn odd,
To ask the ministry of man or god,
But this at intervals for these ten years
Has come back to my mind, sudden as tears,
As if I lay again, too taut to breathe,
Then heard beyond the glass the gentle seethe:
My green physician, waiting out the night
To labour at the alchemies of light.

At The Funeral

Funerals of the old are for the old:
The young, even the middle-aged, intrude,
Stiff in their unpractised piety,
Distracted by oak poppyheads, by light
From stained glass windows blue as irises.
There may be grief, but they are grateful too
To simplifying death that has unpicked
This knot of care from their much-tangled lives.
It is the old that mourn without alloy,
That shoulder loss and lay it to its rest.

Who are they though, so lusty at the back
With lifted voice, needing no book of hymns,
The sad spruce women and the grey-haired men?
What is it that they stare at past the air?
Outside, in winter sunlight, all's revealed:
The cousins of her youth, friends, neighbours, come
To honour old acquaintanceship; now lives
Like long-divided rivers meet again,
A swirling confluence of memory
Carries the dead one to the final sea.

How gently they exclude one. 'That would be
Before your time.' 'That's going back a bit.'
But always to such time they do go back:
To rationing, the Blitz, heroic toil,
The fields of childhood, legendary snows,
Shops, terraces long gone. I understand:
Each dying nerves a new resistance, firms
A final bond of shared exclusiveness.
This is a closing ranks: like pioneers
They man the dwindling circle of their days.

The January sunlight has turned cold.
The ceremony's over. They depart
Down unsafe streets to doors they must keep locked.
What they came to do is done: somewhere
A girl they knew is running over grass
In a green country, leaving them behind
To counters and containments, ritual
And stoic unsurprise, such as they use
Whose lives have fed on long adversity,
Who know betrayal, and will not betray.

From The Train

From the train at dawn, on ploughland, frost
Blue-white in the shadow of a wood.
Oh, you again, of all moods soonest lost
And most elusive and least understood.
What should I call you? Vision? Empathy?
Elation's tunnel? Worm-hole of rejoicing?
Some bliss of childhood, reasonless and free,
The secret microcosms... What a thing
To have no name for, yet to live for, these
Curious contentments under all,
These moments of a planet: weathers, trees –
What dreams, what intimations, fern-seed small,
Are buried in my days, that I must find,
And recognise, and lose, and leave behind?

Geomancies

Like a careful Chinese geomancer
I play the game: *where shall I build my house?*
As if my days and money left more choice
Than standard boxes, twenty to the acre.

Good omens, said that craft, were cradled mound
Within the long blue curve of dragon hills;
A southern upland, where the sunlight falls;
Let water be before you, trees behind,

But keep yourself from pathways that are straight
And shun the level plain, the naked rock
That loose the secret arrows of ill luck ...
O gentle masters of an antique art,

What would you answer now, when all crafts falter?
Where shall we make our dwelling and our path,
Afraid of the deep poisons in the earth,
The sickness in the wind, the death of water?

Sorrow in all lands, and grievous omens.
Great anger in the dragon of the hills,
And silent now the earth's green oracles
That will not speak again of innocence.

Naming The Moths

'You'd call me poet? Hardly, Sir,
    Arms and the man I did not sing,
But once upon an August night
    I named the Yellow Underwing.

'We found on language's great map
    A little corner, left all blank.
Such handiwork, without a name!
    (The Maiden's Blush has me to thank).

'How I recall that dew-damp eve
    Of honeysuckle-scented June
When first upon the Silver Y
    I set the summons of man's rune.

'I see them now, our haunts of old,
    Our hedgerow banks, our woodland glades,
Like memory itself they flit,
    My Early Thorns, my Angle Shades.

'And some, you say, would honour us?
    Then, Sir, I am obliged to you,
But such was never our intent.
    We did what seemed our own to do.

Swifts and Ushers, fold your wings
    Softly on the moonlit land.
They who loved you best are gone,
    Walking somewhere, lamp in hand,

Seeking down eternal lanes
    Moths the angels might have missed,
Proffering before the Throne
    'Some Amendments to Your List'.

Willow Beauty, Burnished Brass,
  China Mark and all the Plumes
With the Footmen gather, dance
  Lightly now above these tombs.

Pen-friend

(for Yang Liuhong)

A girl, a poet, writes to me from China
In quaint uncertain English: in Beijing
Is spring, the trees and grass begin to green
But wind and sand too much, the sky is yellow.
In Beijing autumn is best season: then
The sky is blue, the Fragrant Hill is red,
The Red Leaves red, the mountain is like fire.

Not sure how much she'll understand, I write
In quaint uncertain English back: I say
Here in my country also it is spring,
We have blue flowers underneath grey trees,
The stars last night were bright, I do not know
What stars shine on her country, I am sorry
I cannot write in her own language back.

She sends me poems someone has translated.
Her dreams are white: white coral, moonlight, snow.
Soon, she says, she understand me better,
Then she translate me: I become Chinese.
This grows too strange for my imagining:
Whom shall I meet now, on what fire-red mountain,
Talk with, in what yellow windy spring?

Hedge

They felled the hedge today:
  Hawthorn, tree of twilight,
A green cliff, streaked each spring
  With waterfalls of white.

Now let the voles unlearn
  Their lanes of leaf and bough.
What musty dark will keep
  The hedgehog's secrets now?

And let the birds lament
  Their sanctuary and store,
The redwings that will come
  To the coral feasts no more.

What autumn now shall light
  Their flare-marked landing-strip?
Tonight the hurdling wind
  Forgets its rise and dip.

It is only the eye that stumbles
  At a step no longer there,
The ear, alert, that listens
  For the long surf of the air.

Heatwave

The world's less real on summer afternoons.
We walk in dazzle, wan as daylit ghosts.
The streets are white and foreign: in dim shops
Assistants idle, sheened like melting wax.
In offices, in schools, in hospitals
The hours are burning dunes, and far off yet
Oasis evening with its water-dreams,
Its shadows and its cool solidities.

The countryside's no better: mirages
Sizzle on the surfaces of lanes;
The larks vibrate in poplared distances;
Crops swelter in the fields, on crumbling banks
The soil lips back from blue-white teeth of flint.
All roads are longer: air lies honey-thick
Round farmyard gates; a solitary child
Puddles its naked foot in pavement tar.

Truth is, this is no season for us now:
Untalking and untouching, we endure
Like cattle on the hillside, till day's ebb
Sucks at the round-pooled shadows of the trees.
'For the young' we say, disturbed at light
So riotous and squandered, suited now
To cooler, more reflective husbandries:
Night, and the moonlight's pure economy.

Climbing to the Ridge

A little while, to climb the ridge again:
The body flowing, smooth, on reels of silk;
Wicks of cotton-grass in winter sun
Luminous; red moss; the soil's black butter
Salted with white sand.
                        A little while
To see through wind-gapped mist the fields below
Gleam like ocean shoals, the lake a spearhead
Barbed and tanged with light.
                        A little while
To lie back under white sky; hooded, sleep;
Wake from warm throb to the kiss of snow
And come down-mountain, careless, like a rock-fall.
To say: where does it go?

Beyond the edge of hearing curlews cry.
The pools, wind-shivered, wait for others now.
What is there here to mourn?

Your song is in the silence.
Your stone is on the cairn.

A HOLDING ACTION
2000

The Lame Ant

I have known those who were kindly, not because
They had anything to gain, or thought they had,
Not even, it seemed, from a consciousness of virtue
Or principle of faith; one might have said
Such was their way, from an overflow of gladness
Or because the innocent heart keeps open house
Scorning defence, but anyway, so it was.

I have thought of fairy-stories: how they teach us,
Against all reason, that kindnesses return,
That when the king's son seeks the giant's daughter
What wins the quest is the irrelevant rescue
Of certain wayside ants, who later come
To do the task that he cannot, and gather
The seed the giant has scattered, each last grain.

And I have wondered what part I might play in this,
Knowing myself a grown man, middling hard,
Watchful of my defences, a dour accountant,
Weighing and balancing. And I have thought
That if nothing else I could be one of those
That gather and give back: the lame ant, maybe,
Who brings the last seed in before the nightfall.

Once Upon A Time

The corn-ghost walks at twilight with yellow hair.
In the wood are watching faces, made of leaves.
Set cream for the boggart, silver for the elves.
Beware the black dog on the road, beware
The green-toothed hag of the pond, devourer of men –
So, in an old lost darkness once, we wove
Tales like the firelight, born of fearful love:
A shifting, shadowy propitiation
Of unknown things, the world's fierce otherness,
A lessening of mortal loneliness.

For man is lonely, but the credulous
Have company: fish sing to them from streams,
Birds counsel them, to them the Elf-Queen comes
In her skirt of grass-green silk; it is they who pass,
Bearing their fern-seed, into the fairy hill
For the one night that is seven years beyond.
The feather-cloak is given to the earthbound
And the magic beans are destined for the simple
Who trade their one possession, yet will see
The morning garden green with mystery.

But this was long ago: the world's great childhood
Is over now: those shadows love and fear
Are back within us, where they always were.
They served us well, the goblins of the wood,
The talking wolf, the witch's house of bone,
Taming our night with names, while flowers sprang
Where beauty walked, when the old tales were young.
Now they are done, and we are back alone
On the cold hill, with one true tale to weave
That we shall answer for, and must believe.

The Summer Country

It is August: we are back in the summer country
Caught in a queer sunlit time-warp, watching again
From high cliff paths slow-circling buzzards weave
Their invisible basket of rushes; skimming flat stones
Across a cream-and-turquoise sea; caressing
Lichen's impasto rock-maps; talking late
On honeyed evenings under buddleias,
For this is what we do in the summer country.

We root again in lost simplicities:
Tonight down at the bay I watched the moon
Rise full and hang above the headland, blazing.
The tide was on the turn and wavelets spilled
In scallops of slow silver; when I ran
My shadow flew beside on moonlit sand
In shared immortal fleetness, as if none
Grew old or weary in the summer country.

It is the children belie us: last year's babies
Run up the beach with towels round their heads
Whoo-oo-oo being monsters; toddlers then
Scale rocks; the restless teenagers have gone
Like coracle adventurers. Then we,
Are we not changed? I think, now that I look,
Your auburn hair this year a little whiter.
Is it the sunlight of the summer country?

No, it is telling us: a time will come
When the calm clouds will build above the ridge,
The brassy heads of knapweed nod and shine
Beside the high paths where the buzzards wheel,
The footprints of a wandering breeze will print
A sea of peacock silk, the sun's reflection
Fill trembling pools with trellises of light,
But we shall come no more to the summer country.

The evenings darkening, a touch of frost,
Mist on the sea: love has such hometurnings.
Only, let it endure: let others come
As we have come, each year, to these innocent edges
Where the bruised heart is healed by apple-dreams.
More we do not ask: the bright sand settles,
Leaving clear water as the wave withdraws,
For so it happens, in the summer country.

Accidentals

Fourteen years ago this spring I saw
On a windy day when the white of cherry-blossom
Startled against grey cloud, at the edge of the wood
Where hornbeams grow, a flock of hawfinches
Bold, many-coloured: a gang of swaggering pirates
They dropped from the trees' high rigging with cutlass-bright
                                                    bills
Strutting the leaf-strewn deck; I watched and they
Allowed it: are we ever so honoured as by
Such pure indifference?
                    I have been back
To the wood each spring, but they have never returned.
Life is short for most things: comets, rainbows,
A fall of moonlit snow; one can only be grateful
For the rare conjunctions, for the accidentals
And grace-notes of existence; can only listen
For the once heard, though never heard again.

The Cherry Tree

The cherry tree was doomed, but trees die hard.
It lay beside the woodland path, blown flat
Three months before, the evening of the gale
That threw our beeches down like pick-a-sticks.
That April it still blossomed: you could walk
The whole length of its trunk from airy roots
Through bridal, overarching boughs to find
What only birds by rights had found before:
The secret cave, a waterfall of stars.

The bark of burnished leather peeled like satin.
Look, I said, it's over now, the headsman's
Waited his time, but still she kept composing
Her petalled elegy, that woodland queen,
Putting on, for robe of execution,
The finest of her green gowns, trimmed with lace.

Consider

Consider how they move, the galaxies,
Through the ocean of night like drift nets
Dragging deep space, though nothing we know is there
To be caught in that radiant star-knotted mesh.

Consider how they pass through one another
Like ghost armadas: let the stars be ships
A million miles apart: still that belittles
The loneliness of those bright galleons.

Consider light: by that same token see
A snail-track silverthreading black Saharas
Between the stars, yet nothing anywhere
Outpaces that immortal messenger.

And then consider: who shall know us, what
Companion us: in all the shadowed room
What hands might cup this candle, flickering
In time's wind, in the vast forever dark.

The Remembrance (May 8, 1995)

We crowd the hilltop, standing in loose ranks,
A thousand, maybe, come from all around.

Scents of hawthorn, woodsmoke, trampled grass.
A chilling wind; grey battlements of cloud
Rimmed with gold, pale shafts of hidden fire
Fanwise to the west.
      Eight thirty-three.

A queue for hot dogs; skittish children; prams;
A roped-off bonfire darting orange flames
This way and that, on cold upswirling air.
The minutes tick away. We wait, unsure.

For we were young: what grief was this of ours?
A rumour from beyond the sky, a shadow
That fled before our childhood. Fifty years
Is long for men, in life and memory.
Yet we knew names; we saw the sad closed faces.
Their grief has been our freedom.
       A maroon
Cracks like a whip. A deep obedient hush
Falls on the hill; coats rustle; one small child
Cries and is rocked. We stand. Two minutes pass.
Mist on the plain beneath, a white half-moon
Strengthening above.
      Then bugle notes,
A roll of drums. The solemn statues move,
Speak and are ordinary. We go back,
Torches aloft; cars nose the narrow lane.
Something is served: at least, our silence said
All that the living can say to the dead.

The Visitors

They come like birds of passage now, alighting
To spend the night, not often more; they bring
Girl-friends, babies, gossip, sprawl. The house
Becomes a tidal pool: it fills and empties
While I, unsettled vaguely by that flow,
Patrol my shore, and watch them come and go.

There should be things to say, but what they are
I never quite decide. Should I inquire
After their deepest lives, ask: are you happy?
If they are not, what help now is in me?
So I withdraw from such impertinence
To small talk, or companionable silence.

What could I say to them? Mistrust the glamour
Of unfulfilment: if there is no more
Let things be simple, find your happiness
In gratitude that there should be no less,
Though this, as yet, they would not understand
Who come as migrants now, to foreign land.

No Answer

Grandad, what was it like? Why, it was like
Being young is always: vivid, cruel,
Muddled, ecstatic... should I simply say
It was all a long time ago and I do not remember?
Oh, but I do: we batten down our days
Like a slave-ship's cargo: lift the hatch and there
Huddled incomprehensions stir, a hold
Of human baggage reeks like Africa.

For if the teens were my Renaissance, these
Were my Dark Ages: rank, unchronicled.
My mother was ill and went away; the trains
Made a lonely sound at night; I feared the dark
And had no lamp. Yes, there was kindness too:
But what endures? A brass tap in a playground,
The smell of chalk and milk-crates, rainy mornings,
The tick of boredom, old barbarities.

The grown-up have few choices, but the young
Have none at all: their facts lie all around
But point to nowhere yet, like iron filings
Unmarshalled by the magnet of their power.
Must I explore them then, those unmapped years,
My last white spaces, where the dragons are?
This is no answer, nor yet history:
I have not done with this, nor this with me.

Earth to Earth

Forgive me, most faithful lover, I know you're still making
Gifts to me: today in the meadow it was
A burnet moth in its magician's cloak
Of black and crimson; last night, broken cloud
Around a full moon, rainbowed with its burnish.
Forgive me, then, if I seem to look away
Like one embarrassed by what he cannot repay.

If I said that I was tired, would you understand,
You who never grow tired, whose poems unfold
In the soft thick parchment of magnolia petals,
A guaranteed perfection, old as spring?
You have suffered too, but to be a creature divided
Against itself is a thing you have not known.
For you, all's oneness: water, sunlight, stone.

What my own kind want of me, you would understand,
Knowing their ways, to covet, to consume.
They plough the field of my mind, they harrow me
With sharp needs, make their urgent sowings, reap
Their profitable harvests. But you would have me
Only alert, and fallow, listening
In a dry country for the hidden spring.

Once it was easy to return to you:
When I ran like a fox, and the hunt of the world went by
As I lay in your arms, in the breath of summer bracken.
I loved to run at dusk on grass, barefoot,
Palping the planet, till I dropped and lay
Immortal, melded, watching blue air swim,
Feeling the blood bliss throb in every limb.

Those paths close up, or we abandon them.
Need narrows us, till all our ways are one,
But that leads back: bear with me as I bear,
Holding myself still upright, as I must,
Against your green embrace, your gravity.
As fox to earth at last, to grass the dew,
As love to lover, I shall come to you.

Success

In this overcrowded island
Our lives are like land

And people want them so.
They have crops to grow,

Roads to make, buildings to raise.
So you sell them your days.

It is prison to be poor.
But they want more

Asking 'And what about those
Deep hours like meadows,

Those long days left to lie
For ragwort and butterfly?'

And they come, not once or twice,
Each time with a higher price

As if your stubborn freehold
Were mocking at their gold.

How pleased they are, if you sell.
They call it doing well.

But you, when you contemplate
Time's vanishing estate,

Will you rue the bargains you made?
For this is one-way trade:

Do not think to buy them back,
Those acres that you lack.

Lucre

The river of money has nothing to do with me.
It rises somewhere in the mysterious catchments
Of corporations; debouches, passing me by,
In a broad consumer sea; ascends again
To fall on those rich hinterlands like rain.

How blessed are its waters, which endow
Mortgage companies, missiles, minor royals.
Why have I never knelt in reverence
Beside that trustable transmuting flow?
Indeed, I have heard its voice, seductive, low:

'Not for yourself then: for the desert lives
That you could irrigate, the parching needs
You might have slaked...' And I regret their loss
And mine, or would, but for another voice
That mocks, and cherishes, and leaves no choice.

Limestone Pavement

The sunlit, swarming, coccolithic sea.
What myriads are here, what memory.

Seas drain away, to leave a gleaming skin.
A writing-block. The pens of time begin.

Ice. The stiff stone flexes; eased again,
Cracks and crazes like fine porcelain.

The purest rain is acid. Rocks decay
Where runnelled waters etch the jointed way.

Scribed by that slow calligrapher, each age
Lies lettered on this legendary page.

Sun glitters on the folios of lime
But black with shadow are the runes of time.

Somewhere deep, a murmur like the sea.
What myriads are here, what memory.

The Good Old Days

I'll tell you this, the good old days were cold.
November through to March, our fire was lit
Mid-afternoon, burned up to warmth by evening
When you could get at it for drying clothes
And when it hadn't been put out by falls
Of soot or snow, or else my father burning
Shovelfuls of frozen nutty slack
Scraped from the backyard bunker, or wet logs.

The wind would moan and rattle in the hall.
Doing my homework, six feet from the fire,
I'd freeze on one side, scorch upon the other
Like one of Dante's sinners. Sunday night
Was bath-night; being youngest, I came last
To tepid greasy water heated up
With kettles, while our ancient oil-stove fluttered
Moth-wings of warmth against the icy air.

Going to bed, you shivered for ten minutes
In crackling sheets, curled up your feet away
From arctic nether regions, tried again
And then it came, a warmth at last, like none
A coddled generation can imagine,
A Stone Age bliss, a blood-heat; so you slept,
Waking to winter harvest: sheaves of frost
Heraldic, radiant, on every pane.

The Good Words

If they come less easily, the good words now,
Courage, honour, even love, is it because
We have worn them out with too much make-believe
Or because at last we understand them, how
They bind us to themselves: say 'generous'
And you must give; 'pity' and you must grieve.
Say 'courage', and endure. Always the deed
Proves, or reproves, till we learn husbandry:
Never to use those hoarded words unless
To follow where they lead, finding instead
Virtue enough in sheer necessity.
Yet still the heart remembers 'hope' and 'bless'
And lifts to them, as to a flight of birds
Bound somewhere else, beyond all deeds, all words.

The Birth of Poems

How anonymous, how uncircumstanced are their births.
One forgets they even happened, that at some point
In the workaday time of the world, clouds going by,
Hens in the yard, dogs barking, smoke on the wind,
There had to be a mothering, a making
Of words unmade: 'No longer mourn for me',
'Ah no, the years, the years!', 'Western wind,
When wilt thou blow?', 'So I did sit and eat'.

Yes, one is curious, but they are private
As births should be, hidden beyond recall
In the hollow places of time, in the folds of its silence,
Those lost hours, when the landscape of our love
Stayed as it was for a while: when clouds went by,
Hens scratched, dogs barked, and no-one knew at all,
Except for one who sat, his own sole witness,
Smiling at blank-eyed, inattentive air.

Museum Piece

Not Kensington, this one-room cave of wonder:
I grant you that. Yet where else might you see
Item: a raven's nest, one anaconda
(Stuffed), five Dyak arrows (courtesy
Some late lieutenant-colonel), cannonballs,
A louis d'or, a German silver dollar,
The shin-bone of an ostrich, minerals
(Peacock ore, moss agate, chrysocolla),
An Aztec mask, a curling photograph,
(Young faces, sepia'ed: the Silver Band
In nineteen-twelve), the skin of a giraffe,
And in one corner, quietly to hand,
Item: a proud curator, who's not heard
This world is anything that need make sense,
But sits, contented as a bower-bird,
Selling: 'Museums: Handmaidens of Science'?
Nor is this all: beneath a print, 'The Moon,
Lake Chad', is framed an infant script, addressed
To Mr Bob: 'I liked my afternoon.
I liked it all. I liked the big snake best'.

The Birds

We take it for granted: of course they will always be there
As they always have been, one of those small pivots
Our true lives turn upon, the trustable
Recurrences: I speak of the thrush at twilight,
The robin, the twig-bearing rook, the yellowhammer
Molten on the fence-post at sunset,
The finches clustered on the winter tree
Like red-gold apples: could a time truly come
When the lark did not rise from the green field by the river,
The corn-bunting jangle from wires by the windy crossroad?

Their flight weaves in and out of history
But their time is not ours: there is no mist upon
Their being's bright unalterable lens.
They are like poetry: we come back to them
After years of soil and neglect, as if they needed
No space at all, as if we had only to kneel
For their soaring, perfect, uninvolved absolution
To be bestowed on us. Well, it may be so.
Spring, and the larks are back; the sky, grown rich,
Reverberates around their vanishing.

Dolphin-watching

(For Matthew)

Binoculars cut off the sky and tilt
The green sea like a page; I sit and stare
Watching as if for meaning to appear.
'There!' you say, but it's too hard for me:
The uncoordinated sea yields only
Patches of peacock blue, of wandering turquoise,
Cliff-shadow, cloud-shadow, shoal-shadow; nothing that
                                                    stays.
If only, you say, we had come on some calm evening:
Then in a mirror sea the dolphins barrel,
Leaping in sport. You want me so to see them.
I look again. Was that a fin, that curve?
Nothing for sure. We give up, take the path
Above the high cliffs in the summer wind.
You honour with their names the near at hand:
Purple moor-grass, vetch, the sprinkled gold
Of lady's bedstraw, sea-blue stars of squill.
I taught you once, a little: now you know
Far more than I did then, and I have been
Too much apart from this: I had forgotten
Even the small brown gatekeeper, that lover
Of warm light and the lilac bramble-flower.
No, I could teach you nothing now, unless
A never-disappointedness, to fill
So many days between the dolphin days:
A fallback from the rare miraculous
To earth, and sky, and sunlight on the gorse.

Retirement

Those final years at work:
Like almost drowning,
Which I indeed once did.

Suddenly out of your depth
You find yourself in currents
You can no longer master.

A salt, uncaring sea
Cuffs the strength from your body
And yet, the shore is near.

No, you cannot cry out.
The code of competence
Owns to no need. Sheer anger

Locks your toe at last
To shifting shoal-bank gravel.
You lurch through water, lie,

Spent, at the edge of things,
Spewing up forty years,
Till sunwarmth on your back

Kindles cold flesh; you stir
In core-deep, uncontracted
Wonderment: what now?

One Country

My trade diminishes as yours increases:
I am no nearer to your effortless
Colloquy with the stranger in the train,
To mastering the graceful word that eases
Or the kind word that takes away pain.

I ply my trade by patient circumspection,
Watching for when the soul's door is ajar
And I can slip through like a thief to steal,
But you are welcome there by invitation
Because you go only to give and heal.

Should I resent it then, envy a little
The gift you have I lack and so desire?
Indeed, I could have wished a change of place,
Offered all things to which my craft gives title
For your unstudied, artless human grace.

No, I am only grateful that we form
One country: love knew well then what it did,
Marrying green coast and desert sand,
Your ports of call, your trading posts of welcome,
My watchful, brooding, silent hinterland.

Novices

Such novices we were: what did we know
To marry, to begin a life, start lives?
We had ten pounds between us. Did it matter?
There was love, and for me in those days always a poem
Like a pebble in the pocket, waiting its time
To be taken out again for the slow caressing
Of the mind's thumb, wearing it smooth.
                                                    But what of you:
If I had this, what was it others had
At the rest-point of the mind, the secret place
Where no-one else can come?
                                        It took so long
To understand these things, but watching you
Apprenticed to your own grave crafts of care,
First teacher, mother next, at last I saw
Who kept the centre for me.
                                    And did you
Imagine, for these middle years, your art
Grown effortless, a mastery complete
And never to be lost? They do, the young.
But lovers, parents and poets are always apprentices.
How could that learning end? Now you begin
Again: the grandchild on your lap, and I
Feel something rough against my callused thumb.

NEW POEMS

NEW POEMS

The Programmer's Tale

The mountain men came first: von Neumann, Turing,
Mapping the country, then the pioneers
Following their westward trail; call us
The cowboys then: we lived a brief wild era,
Riders of the electronic range,
Drifters, oddball unemployables,
Coming together on the raw new ranches,
Driving the code-herds up to Abilene.

What was it like? What history is like
For those that live it: sweat and toil, redeemed
By rude self-mocking camaraderie.
No-one, I think, will make a myth of us:
Our skills were real enough, but unheroic,
A kind of naked wit: in languages
Forgotten now as cuneiform we penned
A shadow poetry of pure precision.

And did we see it, what was going on?
A few, not me: for my kind there was only,
Myopic and intense, the task at hand.
An esoteric humdrum owned our lives:
Blizzards of the immediate, dust-storms, droughts.
The bones of abandoned projects whitened the prairies
And yet the job was done: for pride and pay
We built the cyber-world. And then it ended:

The range was fenced, time and the market tamed
Our bright irreverence: we found ourselves
Outlandish among children, old-timers
With campfire stories from another world.
Well, we had had our turn at being young.
Quietly, one by one, we slipped away
Down faded trails, seeking remembered valleys,
The lost, eroded landscapes of the real.

A Candle For Mr Sokolowski

Mr Sokolowski cut hair
In a one-room shop, with till and toiletries,
Chairs and a tall bright mirror. This lit cave
Was Mr Sokolowski's life, this floor
He cleared of its soft sweepings, endlessly,
And these still heads, like heads in prayer, that he
Addressed so fluently, with flashing scissors
And barber's talk, like candle-ends, relit
Smilingly for each new customer:
The match on Saturday, children, the weather.

Who was Mr Sokolowski? Once
A customer spoke of his fussy child:
'Eats nothing'. Mr Sokolowski's eyes
Altered then, I saw it in the mirror.
'You get hungry, eat damn anything.
Ate rat in Russia. Some, worse thing than rat.'
Snip. Snip, snip. The customer's reflection
Nods a surprised and meaningless agreement
And Mr Sokolowski smiles once more:
'So, what you think for game on Saturday?'

Mr Sokolowski shut up shop
Years ago; retired; some seaside place.
Must be dead now: even survivors die
To dream no more of cutting hair, the weather,
The match on Saturday, or other things.

Embassy

It looms like war, this growing old: we live
    On new frugalities of expectation.
The provident have sold up and are gone
    Like refugees from truth's beleaguered nation.
Lady, shall we grow circumspect at last
    And close the embassy of adoration?

The years are baying like a Boxer mob
    And soon enough their pillaging must start.
The documents are all secured, or burned.
    What duty now forbids us to depart
That still we stay, the tattered flag of love
    Unstruck above the refuge of the heart?

Heroic Ideal

'Hige sceal þe heardra, heorte þe cenre,
mod sceal þe mare, þe ure mægen lytlað.'

– The Battle of Maldon

I bet those words were never said at all,
At least not that way. In the thick of battle,
Lead-limbed, parched of lung, swinging a sword
On wet ground treacherous with guts and blood,
A sea of nightmare faces howling hatred,
Your mates decamping, all your leaders dead,
You're likely, right, to spout bravura verse
Polished enough to last a thousand years?
'Let spirits now be harder, hearts be keener,
Let courage be the more as we grow weaker' –
Some Saxon Churchill, then: good leader-work
Dubbed on defeated lips: this was Dunkirk
Without deliverance: we ran and died.
No wonder, then, we looked so hard for pride.

But this I might believe, that in the fight
Some bonehead, unaware of history's spotlight,
Seeing that he had come to the end of his luck,
Muttered the Anglo-Saxon for 'Oh fuck'
And then, among the fleeing, stood his ground.
Whatever. True or not, the words resound,
Unironical, accusing, tough:
Saying not everything, and yet enough.

Beyond

Beyond the god of pure intelligence
Who can calculate, for example, in zero time,
Whether any zillion-digit number is prime
    Stands the god of pure existence
Who does not calculate at all, but knows,
Being in the numbers as in the unfolding rose.

Beyond the god of multiplicity
Who takes for worship all that is defined
By the forever pluralizing mind
    Stands the god of unity
Who says that sun is rose, and rose is sun,
Who is all primes eternally, and One.

Journal

I write in my journal, 'Thrushes in the lane,
A soft wind, and the blackthorn petals falling.'
There would have been much more when I was young:
Each scent of earth, each bird and flower of spring,
But youth is gone, I cannot visit again
The adventure of the blackbird's first song.

And once, I might have wanted to share such words
But now it seems enough that they are for me,
And in time, if time allows, will quicken this day,
Since love, in the end, needs little for memory,
But makes of petals, soft winds, singing birds,
Its momentary, everlasting stay.

Cosmologies

'If you could just keep going in a straight line' –
Said my father, innocent of Einstein,
As we walked home one night of winter stars –
'You'd come at last to somewhere where there was
Nothing at all. I mean, there has to be
A last star, and what then?' This troubled me.
That night in bed I travelled in my mind
Through stars that whirled like snowflakes in the wind
Until I found, beyond one last faint glow,
A blank, like morning fog outside my window.
I woke and cried, but when my father came
To ask what ailed me, was it some old dream,
Sobbed 'Nothing!', so was left to sleep again
Like the blind Cyclops in his cave of pain.

Later I learned: my father had it wrong:
All lines bend back at last, however long.
There is no end to the great blizzard of light
I'd like to tell him now, and so I might
Had he not journeyed on, to somewhere far
Beyond all words of mine, and any star.

Sixty

The dreams of women do not end, but now
All's gentleness: the brushing of bare arms,
A look, the touch of fingers. Strange then, how
If passion's gone I wake out of these dreams
Throbbing with an anguish of desire
Even my youth did not know. A feather's touch
Might lacerate, my body burns like fire.
I cannot sleep again, not after such
Disquietude; I go downstairs, make tea,
Then, as another dawn whitens the garden,
Sit with familiar poets suddenly
Electric, comforting myself with pain,
Caressing words of loss, keener than knives,
Holding ungloved the bright wire of their lives.

Immigrants

Where did they come from? From so many lands.
From mountains, jungles, deserts, snowy plains,
From regions of hot grass, from great slow rivers.
I think there was no country upon earth
That did not send these secret embassies.

Turquoise. Apricot. Mahogany.

How did they get here? In so many ways.
They came in peace and war, with song and story:
Marching in with dusty, sunburnt soldiers;
By caravan along the Silk Road; borne
In white-sailed clippers; carried on the spice wind.
None checked their coming here; no custom-house
Could hinder these that travelled light as air.

Maharajah. Sandal. Talisman.

And did we make them welcome? They were seed.
We gave them earth: some withered, some took root.
At first they tingled on our tongue, like snowflakes,
But then the strangeness melted: they were ours.

Typhoon. Anaconda. Kangaroo.

And will they come again? Never like that.
A language also has its innocence,
Its first fine careless hospitality.
Never again so multitudinous
Those migrants to our shore, like unknown birds
Alighting for the first time, opening
The proud fan of their peacock syllables.

Oleander. Lilac. Cinnamon.

The Craftsmen

In the country of the one-eyed I was blind.
I see it now: I was not good at things,
Or not at things that mattered to my people.
My mind could get no purchase on machines,
My fingers were not apt for tool or brush.
I failed all boyhood's tests: balsa, meccano,
Could offer nothing but a dumb ox strength.
I fetched and carried, glad to be of use.

My craftsmen tribe all but despaired of me,
Decorators, plumbers, carpenters,
Canny and proud, boasting their graduation
From life's university, the school of hard knocks.
They ribbed me for my reading, kind but sharp,
As for some Galilean heresy:
They knew with geocentric certainty
Nothing worth learning ever came from books.

Fifty years on, I hear their accusations
Unanswered still, unanswerable now.
Truly, I bear no rancour: this long quarrel
Is with myself, not them, with my own stubborn,
Impractical, unprofitable craft.
I wonder, though: what if it had been music?
They liked a tune ... we might have met in music,
Or so I tell myself, in unshared words.

The House

Come and live, they said,
In the house of science
With its solid floor of sense,
Its tiled and timbered roof,
Its foursquare walls of proof.

But I chose instead
The house of poetry
Under its rowan tree,
Half ruin and half grave
With green grass like a wave,

Nettles and moss for bed,
And its people coming and going
Like seeds the wind might bring,
Like words in the wind's song,
Their tenancy not long.

The Woods

The woods near my house are strange.
On the map, a few square miles
Penned between road and river.
It should not be possible
To walk all day in April
Through layers of leaf and birdsong
Nor to drift through the long hours
Of summer twilight (outside
Bright fields still giving back
The barley breath of noon)
Yet meet neither road nor person.

And I think of that other wood
Which occupies so few acres
In the country of my life
Yet endures in its own time
And strange geometry,
Where too the familiar paths
Are never quite as remembered
In the shifting dapple of light
As they lead to that adventure
Which is after all only the known's
Illimitable surprise.

To Air

It seems too light a sound
For this invisible benevolence,
This unpraised necessity, like married love,
That makes all things possible.

Better than any wine
Are your vintages to me:
The coolness that distils
In the honeysuckled hollows
Of summer lanes at midnight,
The grey, stone-scented air
Of winter churches at dusk
And the prickle of salt mist
From quiet seas like silk.
I watch by autumn fields
As the plough turns up my childhood
Sharp with raw earth and smoke.

Giver, protector, who tames
Our star's fierce golden furnace
To a whisper of perfect warmth,

Amenable medium,
In whom the ripples of our loneliness
Reach out and meet, in whose domain we build
Our vibrant habitations, music, words,

It is wrong, that litany
That wills us to the grave. The best of us
Does truly go elsewhere.
Think how we hear them, how we shape them still
Over and over, the lost beloved voices
Shelved in your secret libraries. And listen,
That note you always hold, that undersong
Even in silence: earth to earth, it says,
But air to air.

At Steep

(for Myfanwy Thomas on her 90th birthday)

Driving home through Hampshire with my daughter
I see a sign that beckons like a legend
Though on plain earth, and so it is we come
In April twilight, clearing after rain,
Like pilgrim ghosts your childhood might have seen
Out of its unimaginable future,
Up Stoner Hill and round by Cockshott Lane,
To find, through trees and down a root-stepped path,
Your father's boulder, set there on the slope.

My daughter runs ahead of me, downhill
Past dim white cherries, cowslips, violets,
Mildly curious, but wanting tea.

'Who was Edward Thomas anyway?'
I say 'A poet.' 'Oh.' My daughter's twelve,
Likes judo, dancing, being with her friends.
Poems are the things that daft Dads write
Light-years away from coolness.
                                        'Was he good?'
So short a question. And so long an answer
If truth were served: as long, say, as long years
Of looking, loving, waiting.
                                        'He was good.'

I take her photograph beside the stone.
'Can we go back now?' Yes, my love, we can.
To keep the covenant was all I wanted.
You see, this is our obscure faith, our trust,
Whether we live or die too soon, unknowing,
That somewhere in the private rooms of time
Others will read for love alone the words
We wrote for love, alone.
                                        And deeper still
There is another covenant we keep:

Let our words be forgotten, let our lives
Fade utterly, but not these: let there be
Always an April evening, woods, a thrush
Singing and a child, always a child,
A daughter, maybe, finding violets
Or standing in the twilight by a path,
Plucking a bush, with one to see her there
Apart, in all a child's grave otherness,
And love her.
　　　　'Can we get chips?' We get chips.